HITCHED
in 90 Days or Less

by
Linda Gross

To my husband,

Thank you for being the wind in my sail.

Dedications:

This is dedicated to all the ladies who have been single for the last ten years and took it upon themselves to finally find out what it is they are doing wrong.

This is also dedicated to the moms who have begged me to write this book because they are convinced their daughters will never get married (and give them grandchildren).

Prologue:

Men have practically given up on women. It is not because they are commitment-phobic or don't want to get married. It is more that there aren't enough women out there they *want* to marry. Back in the day, men had to marry to have sex. Today, with sex so readily available, men marry because they want to, not because they have to. As such, this has made men much more discerning when tying the knot and they are waiting longer and longer to marry.

Here are some of the reasons they don't marry:

- Men are visual creatures, so as almost everyone in our society keeps gaining more and more weight, some women are instantly dismissed out of the gene pool because most men still prefer thin women.
- Some women are not feminine. They don't know how to let the man lead. Many of our (Women's Lib) mothers told us to not depend on a man and to be strong and independent. While that advice serves us in the workplace, it does nothing for our love life. Ultimately, someone has to lead the dance or you'll have two left feet stumbling over each other.
- Angry, bitchy, and demanding women are not attractive to most men. By watching too much reality television, many women think they deserve the world on a platter without any accountability whatsoever.
- And lastly, many women debase and humiliate their men. In the absence of respect or appreciation, most men will disrespect women in return, most commonly, by cheating.

The upside to this is that all of these negative traits were learned so they can be unlearned to up your odds of finding a great guy.

Women today need this book as they have left the dating pool in droves. 40% of women are single mothers (over 50% to women under 30 years old), which tells me that they have given up on finding a good man. Not only do they not know how to choose a man, they don't even want to commit themselves, as they don't know how. The number of unwed mothers has *tripled* since 1990, according to a nationwide Pew Research Center survey based on data from the National Center for Health Statistics and the Census Bureau.

Never mind that babies born to unwed mothers face an extreme risk of poverty, falling behind in school, and emotional and behavioral problems, today's women are way too selfish to consider those consequences.

Back in the day, teenage girls were schooled by their fathers on how to select good men. Since many children are now raised by single mothers (who abandoned and even forbade any fatherly involvement with their children), young, dating-aged women today need serious intervention and instruction. I wrote this book to bridge that gap.

What is best for our children and future generations is an intact family. There is a seeming 'lack of good men' out there, which is why women today end up with men they are not committed to or don't care for because they believe they have little choice.

When women don't have standards, the quality of the men declines. It's not that there aren't good men out there, it is more that we have allowed men to behave badly. In actuality, the men are just waiting in the wings for you to step it up. They do want to be better men…for the right woman.

It is my goal to get women to understand this dynamic, one woman at a time.

Now, let's get dating!

LINDA GROSS

TABLE OF CONTENTS

Intro

There are hundreds of books on the market about dating. There are probably even a handful of books on how to get a proposal. That being said, there isn't one book on *why* men do or do not ask the girl to marry him.

After having interviewed **20,000 men** and being a Gender Differences Expert, this book is largely based on how men think. Knowing how men think allows you to position yourself favorably for marriage.

Post Women's Lib, I think many of our moms raised us to be Amazon women thinking that we can do it all. While this advice works well in the workplace, it doesn't give us the best shot in our personal lives. Many young women today don't have the foggiest idea of how to be feminine. In fact, they view femininity as a relic from the past and something to be avoided. They view femininity as being weak. Well, nothing could be further from the truth.

There is great power in being feminine. Of course, no one wants or benefits from domination/submission and it is not what this book is about. There are certain traits that are naturally attractive to men. True femininity is about being alluring and magnetic. I will teach you some of these behaviors that you can use to attract your dream guy.

Enjoy the ride!

DT (Short for Dating Tips.)

Definition of the word HITCHED in this context:
To get a *proposal* within 90 Days or Less.

I recommend a standard engagement period, one year, to actually get married.

Almost Every Guy

I have dated,
Proposed To Me
in
Three
Dates.

Now, I'm not going to hold you to that standard. I am going to give you all the insider tips as to why I think that happened to me…repeatedly and consistently. If you follow my guidelines, you should be getting a proposal within 90 days.

Women are fast. Men are slow. Women know within 5-15 minutes of the first date if this guy is a good contender. Unlike women, men don't think in terms of relationships. Men have an agenda and their top agenda is not a relationship, like it is for us. Women are hard-wired to be in a relationship, as it is easier to have a kid when there is a man there to help you emotionally, physically, and financially. That's why women seek relationships.

Monogamy is inherent for women. Monogamy is not inherent for a guy. A guy has to talk himself into monogamy, especially today (since sex is so readily available). Marriage was originally intended for the benefit of women and children. At first glance, there is not much in marriage for a guy. Men are waiting longer and longer to marry. As of this writing, the average age a guy first marries is now 28 years old. Also, fewer men are marrying at all.

In the 1920's, 92% of women would get married. In the mid-1970's, due to the invention of the Pill and the influence of Women's Lib, marriage rates for women crashed and hit an all-time low of 76%. The rate has been on the decline ever since. In 1980, for census statistics for men over 35 years old, 6% of men remained unmarried. In 2010, that number shot up to 14%.

Before the invention of the Pill in the late 60's, men got married because they had to. In order to get sex, they had to get married. Today, because sex is so readily available, men don't have to get married. Men get married because they *want to* not because they have to.

Generally speaking, most women still want a relationship. That's how they are programmed. Generally speaking, most men (18-35) don't. This is a crucial point for women to understand why men don't want to marry (because there is not that much in it for him. Remember, marriage was invented to protect women and children).

There are some guys who are interested in marriage before the age of 35. Generally speaking, these are guys who are lazy and don't want to "go on the hunt" to find sex all the time. They figure if they marry one person, sex will be readily available. This assumption is not true, but that is the premise from which these men are operating.

When a guy can get sex without monogamy, why should he get in a relationship with you?

> *The answer to that is that you have to be so irresistible to him that he cannot NOT marry you.*

The goal of this book is to make you irresistible. Let's get started.

Why You Should Say "No".

In my twenties, I was in four multi-year relationships. During this this decade, I just didn't want to get married or, more honestly, they were good enough to date but they didn't have the something special that made them irresistible to me. That's why I didn't pull the trigger. My mom and dad were married for a long time because they were old school, but they were so miserable and were not well suited. I didn't want to end up like them. They were each fabulous in their own right, but toxic together. So, I waited.

Anyway, back to the story. I lived with one of the men for six years, lived in my own place with two of the men, and was engaged (but I called it off), to the fourth man. Each of the four men above proposed on the 3rd date. Because I am an honorable person, I always gave the ring back. They all refused to take the ring back (see what happens when you're irresistible?). One person, the one I was engaged to but called off one month before the wedding, actually said "No, you keep it. It's been an honor knowing you."

After this initial fiancé, I kept getting more and more proposals and rings. It got kind of embarrassing. Finally, I got married in my thirties and was married for a long time (another proposal on the third date and married four months later). After my marriage ended and I got back onto the dating scene, I assumed, at almost 50, I no longer had the "IT" factor. I assumed wrong. I was still getting proposals. I made a decision to not go out with the same man more than two dates (since they always seem to propose on the third date) unless I really, really wanted to be with *this* guy.

Newly single, I went on 73 first dates (my choice, I dumped most of them after the first date). I had terrific times and had talked to them at least for 2-4 weeks before the actual date, but they weren't the right fit for me. A few I told I could be just friends, if they agreed, but not a love interest. They understood and still wanted to hang around. Of the 73 dates, I went on a second date with three of them. I am married now to one of those three. On the third date, we were at a large gathering and he told all his friends he loved me (ahead of saying it to me). I think we went ring shopping on the fourth or fifth date.

Remember I said that I didn't want to get married in my twenties? They were all terrific guys. My friends accused me of being too picky, so in my thirties, I let down my standards and dated a wider selection of men. In hindsight, this was not a good idea at all. After all, I wasn't marrying for my friends' standards but for my own. I had to make me happy, not them. After marriage, the more I said "no", the easier it got to end it after the first date.

Women are generally people pleasers, often to the detriment of themselves. What I learned in saying "no" was that I kept getting closer and closer to what I wanted and needed. That would have never have happened otherwise. I kept my responses classy. For example, I would say something like, "I had a wonderful date and you're a great person, but I don't feel the 'click.'" People cannot argue with a feeling. You either feel something or you don't. Like I say, women are pretty fast at figuring if this is the guy or not. Do the gut check and stick to it.

Women do the gut check but often ignore it and talk themselves into staying with the guy. Don't do that. If you don't want to be with a smoker, don't be with a smoker. If you don't like his line of work, for example his being a policeman scares you that he might not come home, don't be with him. It doesn't make him any less of a person. He is just not right *for you.*

Women often date the guy for six months because they are lonely or want free meals, only to dump the guy later. It is wrong to take advantage of someone's good nature. Good character brings good character. Don't abuse men (and they won't abuse you).

The upside to saying "no" quickly is you really learn a lot about yourself. You learn what makes you happy, and isn't that what life is about? Finding happiness? It is.

The more you say "no", the more the universe throws out new and different variables (for you to decide on). With each step, you get closer to your true self. That journey alone is worth the price of admission!

Saying "no" is hard at first but gets easier with practice. The key thing to remember is to always be classy, always be a lady, and always honor the great in them. It's a bit like ice cream. No one should tell you what flavor to like. Either you like vanilla or you don't. That doesn't mean there is anything wrong with chocolate or pistachio or cherry. Each person is entitled to their own likes. Own what you like or don't like about this guy and use that as your guide. Ignore the pressure from the guy, your mom, your friends, and whoever else wants to butt their head into your business. You know what you feel and that is all that matters. In fact, it's the only thing that matters.

Saying "no" leads to more and better "yeses".

My Notes:

My ACTION LIST:

Smile.

The best enticement you can use is to smile.

A smile means "come here". A smile means you're approachable. A smile means you're available.

Most men, no matter how cute you are, are super terrified to approach a woman without getting a sign from you that it's safe to come over. A smile does that and then some. When you are out, remember to smile!

***

Since eye contact and smiling go hand in hand, I'm going to give you a tip on eye contact. Most people hold their gaze for one to two seconds. If you can hold your gaze on someone for three to five seconds, you can actually make someone's heart race. This longer-than-normal gaze is quite magnetizing. It's almost like he "has" to come over to you. Six seconds or longer is creepy, especially for someone you don't know. Three to five seconds is ideal.

The three to five seconds are best combined with your looking down or putting your chin down (like you're shy) after the five seconds. You can also look up and to the right after the five seconds (like "uh-oh, I got caught"). Both techniques are very alluring and flirty. In Neuro-Linguistic Programming (NLP), this construes imagery and visual fantasy, meaning that you are "imagining" being with him. It's very effective. Girls today are so busy being like men (obvious and direct instead of inferred gestures) that they have lost the art of being feminine and flirty. This is a step in that direction.

Beyond this, smiling people are usually happy people…and who doesn't want to be around someone who is happy?

My Notes:

My ACTION LIST:

He Won't Ask Me Out.

Oh, girl? Don't you know! I dealt with this in my twenties and thirties.

A little of this is because of him.

a. Many men today were raised by single mothers who told them "the sexes are the same". You don't have to walk over to her/ask her out because there is a good chance she will walk over here/ask you out or whatever. To that I say bullshit. Any man worth his salt will move mountains, no matter how shy he is, to come to you. You don't want a man who will not come to you. It means he is afraid. It means he won't take a risk. It means he does not want to face rejection. So what? It's part of being a man. A real man will acknowledge the feeling of possible rejection but will walk over to you anyway. The reward overcomes the risk.

   If you have to chase him, he isn't the right kind of guy. He is not man enough. You want a man who is 'man enough'. Man enough to at least come over and try.

b. He needs an invitation from the Queen. Hmmmph! He can't possibly come over because he has to check with all his male herd to see if they know anything about you. After he has squeezed them dry for the information about you, he needs to also find out IF you might like him. He is minimizing his risk (in case you reject him). He thinks he is being smart, but he is really just being a wimp to avoid risk at all costs. Again, not the kind of man you want. You want a man who takes a risk when the situation calls for it. If there is a tsunami, earthquake, or a riot, you want the person who will lead you to safety.

   This is a strange dynamic. When I go to Europe, men ask me out the moment I set foot on the pavement outside my

> hotel. I hate to admit this, but sadly, I think this 'mother-may-I' attitude is strictly an American affliction.
>
> There really is nothing you can do about this deterioration of manliness other than to tell women to not raise their sons by themselves. Sons need male influence. If the dad is not around, she needs to bring the son around his uncle, grandfather, sports coach, religious affiliation, or other male mentors.

A little of his not asking you out is because of you.

What I am addressing is he likes you but he still won't walk over here/ask you out. This book will teach you why this occurs. Mainly, it's due to your not be receptive enough (feminine) to be inviting. Pay close attention to the following chapters:

- Smile
- You wear too much black
- Date 100 men
- Don't tell him what you want
- Get rid of the extra men in your life
- Don't make him second banana to your son
- If you can control him, dump him
- If you can't root for him, let him go
- Magnetic. Be cute, be chill, and fun to hang out with

and most important of all of these:

- You need to need him

Also, be aware of who might be cock-blocking his efforts. Your male best friend? Your mom? Your (jealous) girlfriend?

Bottom line? You need to be open to having him in your life. If you are putting up unconscious roadblocks, and they can range from your weight to your career, to your money, to goodness knows what, it will serve you to figure out what those roadblocks are. Commit to a timeline to remove them from your life.

My Notes:

My ACTION LIST:

Road Blocks, Cock-blocks, and Other Signs.

A girl may have the best intentions when she starts dating, but subconsciously she may be doing things that are sabotaging her chances of success. Many of these behaviors are below the surface and not in your awareness. You need to reach deep and/or ask for help to see these behaviors that block you.

a. Male friends. One of the easiest and most effective changes you can make is to remove your "extra" heterosexual, "male best friends". See the chapter below for more info on this.

   Look at it this way, you don't like him enough to go to bed with him or consider being in a relationship with him. Isn't that enough to tell you what direction you should take this? If not, keep asking yourself this question.

   From your *new man's* point of view, the 'male friend' is a hanger-on. He's not man enough to close the deal with you (do you really want someone who can't close the deal?) but he is *hoping* you will notice what a great guy he is and that YOU will close the deal.

b. Him. Yes, him. You are stuck on your old boyfriend. Ya, I'm sure he was all that. That being said, it ended or never got off the ground in the first place. There was a reason for that. Relationships are supposed to be easy. When they aren't, there is a reason. Spend a day or two and analyze what you did wrong (OR what he did wrong) and move on. Don't let this person be a placeholder for the awesome man who awaits in your near future.

c. The meddlers. This could be your mom, your (jealous) girlfriends, your frenemies, your co-workers, etc.

   Sure, getting advice is good, but there comes a point in time when their "good intentions" may not be working for you.

They may be holding you back, keeping you from your true self, and stopping you from finding your person.

For years, friends and family used to tell me that I was 'too picky'…and I listened. One day I woke up and decided, guess what? Am I marrying this person *for them* or for me? Maybe that person would have passed muster for their standard but not for me. It was when I realized that I could ask for more then I got more. Read that again because it's important.

d. Baggage. You know, baggage. You make excuses because you need to lose a few pounds, you're not young enough, you don't make enough money, you're not pretty enough, your parents had a rotten marriage, your dad was not in the picture when you were growing up so you don't know how to pick a man.

Basically, you're one excuse from finding him, so, whatever it is, drop your baggage at the doorstep. It will still be there tomorrow. You can deal with your issues another time. For now, for today, you are worth it. You're worth it because I said so. You're worth it because you want to be happy. You're worth it because you are ready to find him.

There is an added bonus to taking this approach: momentum. By doing something good for yourself, you put things into perspective. It may just be the approach you need to get off the dime and start solving some of the problems that are dragging you down.

Action cures depression. I'm not saying to ignore your other problems. They will still be waiting for you. I'm saying to give them less attention, for now. Do something positive for yourself. Once you're in a positive frame of mind, you can more easily deal with those old issues.

My Notes:

My ACTION LIST:

Change Your Routine.

Studies have shown that by hitting the 'refresh' button on your daily grind leads to a better love life and greater job satisfaction. It goes without saying that changing things up also helps with dating.

- Try a different coffee shop.
- Shop at the market across town.
- Walk around the courtyard in the office building next door (not your own).
- Go to the gym at 5pm, instead of 7pm.
- Go out with just one girlfriend or even alone, instead of with five other people. Studies show men are more apt to approach you if you are alone or with just one person.
- Walk your dog on the weekend at 7am instead of 8am.

The key here is to break up your routine.

Sure, you might experience different feelings: fear, discomfort, and/or it might be inconvenient. That's perfect normal. Just feel the feeling and do it anyway.

What can be better than meeting fresh new faces, going to new places, and doing new things? It really is fun…if you let it be. Exploring new environments and situations releases dopamine (the feel-good hormone). This drives learning and may even slow down aging. Simply *looking* at pictures of new places (where to go) and new people (his profile or seeing new men in person) spikes activation in your brain's pleasure and cognition centers. With new places and people, you are forced to process new experiences. This stimulates your brain's reward centers and stimulates your gray matter, which helps memory and lessens your chance for getting Alzheimer's!

View every outing as you bursting out of your shell, even if, and especially if, the date doesn't work out. This is not about *him*. This journey is about finding yourself, what works for you and what doesn't. In the end, you will be better for taking this trip.

My Notes:

My ACTION LIST:

Create Space/Feng Shui

Feng Shui is the Chinese philosophical system of harmonizing everyone with the surrounding environment. The term *feng shui* literally translates as "wind-water" in English. The wind is male energy (Him) and the water is feminine energy (You).

So how does this ancient philosophy apply to you? Well, take a studied look at each and every corner in your house. If you had a marriage-worthy man living there, how would the placement of objects/furniture be different?

For me, I had end tables but the second (his) end table was in another corner of the room being used for another purpose. I had to clear away the room on "his" side of the bed to place the end table (his) back in its rightful place. I love to read at night. I had a reading light on my side. I had to buy another reading light for his side. Meaning, I wanted a man who is well-read…like me.

As you look around each room, make sure objects are matched and in pairs, allowing for a mate in your life. If a picture or artwork is a "single", see if you can replace it with something depicted as a couple.

Since my dining room was rarely used, somehow had become a junk storage area for odds and ends. I cleared out the whole room and started over. I put the leaf back in the dining table to return the seating to a table for six. I bought a pretty tablecloth. I removed all objects that didn't belong in a dining room. I bought a pretty framed poster showing a couple dancing. With my new boyfriend, who later became my husband, I started a new tradition. Every Wednesday, I made a gourmet meal. We dubbed this our "Wednesday Night Dinners." I was the chef. I planned the meal, I did the marketing, and orchestrated the meal. My guests and new boyfriend (who also could cook, by the way!) were my sous-chefs as I had them chop or stir. By some karmic magic, putting the leaf back in the table created a magnetic attraction for people wanting to fill those seats! There was a waiting list for people who wanted to come over for Wednesday Night Dinners!

So look around and see what you can change. One lady I spoke with bought a recliner for her living room with a side table with some men's books on it (as she wanted a reader). Another woman made some space in her medicine cabinet. She put an extra toothpaste tube, toothbrush, a razor and some shaving foam in that space. Another woman made space in her liquor area. She bought some good scotch and put it on a display tray along with two manly scotch glasses, a small crystal ice bucket, and a pair of ice cube tongs hanging off the side.

The tenets of feng shui say that everything has an energy, a vibration if you will. If you create a vibration for your future man to be attracted to your space, you will draw him into your world.

Go create your man-space!

My Notes:

My ACTION LIST:

You Wear Too Much Black.

Wear black to a funeral. Black is depressing.

Black means you don't feel good about yourself that day. Black means you're bloated and want to hide.

I think I wore black probably 80% of the time in my twenties, until one guy explained to me how a guy interprets a girl wearing so much black. No guy wants to date a girl who is depressed, and to a guy, black represents depression. Guys want to date a girl who is fun to hang out with and too much black/goth (along with makeup, accessories, boots, etc.) is the antithesis of that.

That 'simple black cocktail dress'? Sure. It's for an hour or so, every few months. Now as I'm typing this, I realize that I have thirty such 'simple black cocktail' dresses. I have got to weed them out! Note to self, pare it down to six.

If it's not a funeral or suggested 'cocktail' attire, experiment with color. Color takes effort. Do the accessories, shoes, and makeup match? Color implies you are happy (whether you are or not). And sometimes, just wearing color makes you happy. (Where you weren't a few minutes before wearing it. How cool is that?)

Wearing color makes you have a little attitude and a little attitude is good. You have to 'own' what you wear. When you do, that confidence will shine.

Well? Are you color dead? Here is how we are going to e-a-s-e into it:

The bottoms (skirts, pants, and shoes) are going to be these 3 colors: white, beige, and black. Your tops, dresses, accessories, and (subtle) makeup will be in color. Almost all colored items go with white, beige, and black, so you can't go wrong. Do this for a few months until you graduate to going for a mixed use of color, looks, and patterns.

A good way to graduate?

- Enlist your friend who is a super-fashionista. She's dying to help.

- Ask a personal shopper, like at Nordstrom, to help you. They are free.

- Grab a few young magazines, like Marie Claire, Glamour, and In Style. Stay away from the haute couture magazines like Vogue and Harper's Bazaar. No one dresses like that in real life. The fashions are more for editorial layouts than what a normal girl can pull off.

- Empty out your closet completely and put the contents on your bed. You need to do spring cleaning anyway. Invite your 'Martha Stewart' type friend over and make some cocktails. Set aside the bottoms that are white, beige, and black. Those are you "go-to" items. Group the colored items together with clothes that are in the same color. Group the items by type, i.e. short-sleeved shirts with short-sleeves, sweaters with sweaters, jeans with jeans, etc. Now you can actually "see" what you have. This will make your job 100% easier.

  Whatever you are not going to use: give away, trash, or donate.

Life is not dark and dreary. You are going to find a man. As you lighten your colors, your world will lighten up just a bit. It might just be the little push you need for him to find you. A little red never hurt anyone. It might be enough to get you noticed and he might soon be walking over here before he can say "Ay Carumba!"

My Notes:

My ACTION LIST:

Have a Type.

Men have a type and so should you. There are men who like redheads. There are men who like girls with glasses. There are men who like women with long legs.

Too often, I hear women say they don't have "a type". I don't know, but you just sound ridiculous when you say this. Saying this aloud sounds lazy and resigned.

If I were to translate the 'girl-speak', I would say it means "I really don't know what does it for me. I will just take what comes along. After all, it's about his personality, right? If I don't like what I see, I guess I can work on him to change it, right? People can change for the better, right?"

Like I say, it just doesn't sound right. Men do not resonate to women who talk like this and they certainly don't appreciate a woman trying to change them.

Let's put this in terms of a job. If you were to go to school to be an x-ray technician, you put in your time, you put in your money, you sacrificed your fun time because you had to study, et cetera…when you get out of school, there is no way you don't have in mind what "type" of job you are going to get. You're not going to get a job parking cars, right? You're not going to take a job being a waitress. You're not going to take a job being a stripper, right? And if you are smart, you likely will get an internship in your field or a closely related field while you are getting your schooling done. Well, why aren't you taking this approach with a guy? Exactly.

I hate to say it, but only a girl with no skills takes just any job (because she is not qualified otherwise). Likewise, a girl who takes 'just any guy who comes along' screams that you are needy and have no direction in life.

If you are not a smoker, a smart girl would not take on a guy who is a smoker. If you have a degree, a smart girl would not take on a stupid or an unambitious man. If you have manners, a smart girl would not take on a guy who is uncouth or unkempt.

No type? I don't want to hear this talk anymore. You're the girl he wants to marry. Act like it. Start making your list of what you will and will not accept in a man. If someone comes along who doesn't make the grade, politely, and in a lady-like way, toss him back in the stream.

He is not a home improvement project. You are not his mother. You want someone who is already grown.

You're better than that. Get with someone you would be proud of.

My Notes:

My ACTION LIST:

Never Fish Off the Company Pier.

You've heard it once, you have heard it a million times. Some companies even have a policy against inter-office dating. Don't date men in your office.

I don't agree with the following:
"Familiarity breeds contempt."

To me, the more appropriate saying should be:
"Familiarity breeds sex."

Spending a third of your waking hours in the office makes you get to know the people you work with very well, sometimes even more than friends or family. That level of familiarity lends itself to 'liking' someone. "Gee, we work so well together." "We understand what the other person needs to get this project done." "We complete each other's thoughts/sentences."

I get it. Who wouldn't fall in love with that level of understanding?

That being said, if you value your job and your money, which really means you value YOURSELF, you would not put yourself in jeopardy by dating this man. Dating this man might lead to breaking up with this man. This causes not only hard feelings for you, but it causes disruption (or jealousy) in the office during and after the time you are dating. The situation may get so thick, you might get fired. You really do not want to get fired. It's not pretty.

Unless you can easily transfer to another branch or location, or you have just put in your two weeks' notice to quit, I wouldn't recommend taking this risk. The downside trumps the upside. Keep looking.

My Notes:

My ACTION LIST:

Date 100 Men.

I was married for a long time. When I got on the dating scene after my divorce, everything that I knew before was practically obsolete, mainly because of the arrival of the internet. The good thing is the internet made our world smaller and more accessible. To make it through the tide, I had to learn new rules.

Along with the positives of being able to connect with more people came the negatives. People could readily lie and deceive behind the safety of a keyboard. Back in the day, we had one telephone with an answering machine and one physical address. Now it is not uncommon to have six email addresses, a post office box (which is not even at the post office), and at least a half a dozen social media accounts. Add in easy Google searches to the mix and the internet can either be your friend or foe.

One common thing I notice about people who are stuck, (*that was me, too, by the way*) is they are searching for perfection. Forget about 'finding Mr. Perfect'. This step is to get <u>you</u> to just...start…dating! Don't overthink it. It's simple! All you have to do is date 100 men.

You cannot attract Mr. Right if you are not yet right yourself. You will find this task to be more about learning about YOU than it is about finding *him*. The bonus is…you *will* find him. Let's get started.

During my dating quest, I tried a number of things:

- Going out with my girlfriends and meeting new people in person.
- Speed dating.
- Lunch dates for singles.
- Happy hours for singles.
- Wine tastings.
- Fun destination vacations.
- Blind dates.
- Other people's backyard barbecues.
- Asking other people in my industry if they knew anyone.

- Playing sports.
- Sporting events.
- Taking classes.
- Online dating.

I'm probably forgetting what else I did, but it seems I tried them all. Along the way, I read a magazine article that got the job done!

Get yourself out there! Men are not going to find you holed up in your apartment. I would recommend also doing many of the items listed above. I spent anywhere from $5 to $1,000 doing the above activities, mostly with spotty results.

Here is the tip I read that did it for me: Date 100 men! And date, I did. I figured 'this is pretty doable'. I will continue to do my above activities and not settle unless it's someone I really want to see again.

Because I usually get proposed to on the third date, I figured I would take that out of the equation and not let it get to the third date...unless I made a conscious choice to go out with them again.

I had a gut check with each date and if I couldn't see myself long term with that person, I let him go.

I know that is counterintuitive to women as most women like going out to dinner or a movie or nice event. It's not even about the guy, it's going out that attracts most women. Do not be a typical woman. Don't go out with him just because you got a nice/free meal out of the deal. Learn to say 'no'. Your time is more valuable than some silly dinner.

I would say that most of my dates came from online dating. After they contacted me (he has to take the risk, not me. I didn't choose him, I let the guy be the guy and pick me. It's more worthy that way), I would pre-screen them for about two to three weeks before the actual date.

Remember that the phone and the internet are pretty much all fake. Almost everyone sounds/looks good on the internet/phone. Do not spend a long time talking to him. You want to MEET him. Make the interactions short, maybe five to ten minutes. Again, if he exhausts everything about you, he is not as motivated to actually make the date. Also, keeping the interaction short keeps his interest high. You're available but a bit mysterious (by not being so available). I would say it's ok to have only one or two long calls, like an hour, just before meeting him.

Absolutely avoid any call that is going to go on for hours and hours on end. It likely means he is attached to someone else. Otherwise, he'd be planning the date already.

<u>The most crucial skill I had to learn</u> for online dating was sniffing out the married guys. Be very wary as a disproportionately high number of 'desirable' guys on the internet are married. Of course, you cannot come right out and ask if he is married, because he will LIE. Use your female intuition and listen for red flags. I became really skilled at sleuthing out discrepancies and so should you.

I often went out on five dates a weekend. Forget the nonsense about how a woman should only date one guy at a time. I did not go to bed with these guys, but I DID date multiple guys. This is one trait about dating that I would say 'date like a guy' and date multiple people. Date like it's a job search because in essence, it is. You wouldn't just send in one application in your job search, right? You would send in as many as possible in your field, hoping you get two or three good possibilities. The same rule applies here.

I had one Friday, Saturday, and Sunday night dates and Saturday and Sunday morning dates for the guys who weren't at the top of my list, totaling five dates a weekend. Every once in a while, if I didn't have five dates stacked up, I would date on a Tuesday or Wednesday night.

How did I get that many dates? Be what guys mostly want. Men's criteria are typically:

- Are you cute?
- Are you chill?
- Are you fun to hang out with?

Usually in that order.

Just because most girls don't care much about (his) looks, guys do care about what YOU look like. Try to look cute as often as possible. This means not too much makeup, too much perfume, and wear something that shows you have a waist. If you go lower on the neckline, go easy on the hemline, and vice versa. Less is more. Look like the person he would be happy to introduce to his friends or family should you accidentally run into them.

As for your profile, take pictures, good pictures, discarding the ones with poor lighting and unattractive facial expressions. Take pictures often. I took selfies before selfies were even possible or popular. My camera had a self-timer. I would set up the shot and I would have 10 seconds to jump into the shot. It might take a couple of takes to get used to doing this, but it's worth it. If you don't have a lot of friends who will keep taking pictures of you, it's something to add to your repertoire.

If you have no sense of style, I would consider going to an upscale store like Nordstrom's and let them give you a makeover. You want to keep it simple. I do not recommend going to MAC or those glamour makeup makeover stores in the mall because they tend to go overboard. Most men do not like excessive make-up on women. They like a little makeup, so it enhances your natural beauty, but not so much that you would scare the bleep out of them if they saw you in the morning (with no makeup).

Men like action shots (because they can imagine doing fun things with you). "Here I am roller skating with my friends." "Here I am going away for the weekend." "Here I am going out on the town."

Keep the pictures clean. Remember, you are classy, not scandalous. You want to present yourself as attractive and marriage-material. If at all possible, show your waist (keep elbows away from your waist so he can see the outline). Also, for the same reason, don't wear clothing that is like a tent (and makes you look pregnant).

Women generally like face shots because they are trying to read clues about his personality. Conversely, men like full-body shots as they want to visually see if you are fit and/or someone they are attracted to.

Today's selfie style generally isn't going to work with men. Why? Because it only shows the distance between your arm and your face. Like I said above, men want a full-body shot. Consider adding an app that adds a 10-second delay to your smart phone camera shot, so you can get into the shot. Put a giant legal clip at the bottom of your phone (to hold it upright) and hit the timer. There are also inexpensive accessories that will cradle your phone to remain upright for a couple of dollars.

Aside from using the delay feature, you will have to keep asking your friends or strangers to take a picture. If you have your friend or a stranger take the shot, always have them take two shots. The first one might not be the best one.

Get good at evaluating your pictures. Don't post every picture you take. Remember the shot should answer the question: Am I cute? Am I chill? Am I fun?

If the shot doesn't answer one or more of these questions, put them in your personal album but not on the online dating profile.

***

Like that old shampoo commercial said "Wash, rinse, and repeat." I kept at it until I found someone that I wanted to go on a second date with. Out of 73 dates, only three people got a second date. Out of those three, I ended up marrying that last person.

After going on a dozen dates, I realized that this process had very little to do with picking the guy and more to do with ME! That was a very deep revelation. It was a lesson for me to learn how to say "no". I had to level with myself to figure out just "what is it that I do want?"…and then have the guts to go after it. It was a giant lesson in "I DO MATTER". This is why this step worked so well and on so many levels. I trust that this step will awaken your true self as well.

Another bonus? By being in what I call 'active dating mode', you are sending the universe the message that 'I am in active dating mode'. The universe keeps sending you more and more quality guys, a Law of Attraction, if you will. The more you heighten your awareness of something (It is like buying a new car. You now notice every new car that is the same make, model, and color as yours.), the more of that 'something' you receive in your world.

Like I say, this process is not so much about him. It's about changing YOU. You will change by doing this exercise. Your changing brings the right guy closer and closer to you.

This lesson is also a lesson on being a lady. Don't be rude and obnoxious when rejecting guys. Don't be unresponsive and ditch the guy. This poor behavior muddies the waters and will impede your progress. You want to reject guys gently and with class. That is a learning step, too. No guy wants to be with a woman who is a jerk. He figures, sooner or later, you will be undignified to him, too (and he is right). Guys are attracted to women with integrity. Lady-up and be a good person always.

My Notes:

My ACTION LIST:

Meet and Greet. 1st Date Law.

The first date should be short and sweet. Period. End of story. With NO exceptions.

I can't tell you the number of people who have told me that they thought the date went great because it lasted 5 or *X* (fill in the blank) hours. Guess what? Those people are still dating or have already been dumped by the time you read this book. I know what I am talking about. Just do it.

The first date should be one hour and not a minute more.

If you can't figure this out, set your phone alarm to ring in an hour. Have your friend call you in an hour. Actually schedule another appointment that you cannot miss forcing you to leave in an hour. Whatever method you use, just do it. Limit the first date to no more than one hour.

This step is not a 'suggestion'. It is Law.

Why is this rule so important?

1. Click or no click?

If you end up not liking the person in person, you can leave graciously. No harm, no foul, as they say. It is my experience that practically everyone sounds good on the phone or on a text. The real test is getting them in front of you. Either you guys click…or you don't. It's that simple. Pay attention when you meet them.

This yardstick (click/no click) should be the only aspect of the date that you are evaluating. Aside from that, just let it flow and have fun.

If you are not feeling it, be gracious, be a lady, and politely end it. Sometimes, you can do it at the end of the date, other times, you may not know until the next day. That's ok. You really should deliver the news within 24-72 hours, tops.

Say, "I really had a good time. You're a good person. I just didn't feel 'the click'. Good luck in your search." Done. Short, sweet, and to the point.

Having a short, first date is a good plan for many reasons. Your time (and money…gas, parking, new outfit, and whatever else you paid for to go on this date) is kept to a minimum.

If the date doesn't work out, neither of you is invested, which makes it a perfect time to exit. I have talked to hundreds of women who wait six months to tell the guy she is not interested. That's unacceptable behavior…not to mention, cruel. Most women know in fifteen minutes. There is no reason to drag this on for six months or *any* number of months. At that point, you are just using the guy for a free meal or however else you are manipulating him. I don't approve. It's not classy. And men don't marry women who are not classy.

2. You clicked! Hooray!

Most women at this point will say, "We clicked, so even though we followed your one-hour rule, we extended the date by going somewhere else to continue the date."

To which I say, "Well, you didn't follow my rule."

If you clicked, you should still end the date. Why? Because you want to leave him wanting more. I often get an invitation to schedule the second date at the close of the first date. That's how you KNOW you are doing it right. It is okay if he doesn't ask right away, but he should ask within 72 hours. If he doesn't, he is usually playing you, and you don't want a player. (Translation: 90% of the time, he is married. 10% of the time, he is undecided and otherwise unavailable). Move on.

Never be the one who decides if there is a second date. Let him be the man. In the beginning stages of dating, it's always good to let the man lead. If you are doing the asking, you will never really know if HE likes YOU. He may say "yes" because he is lonely, bored, or horny. <u>It does not mean he likes you</u>. And in today's modern world, he may be using you for money, power, connections or whatever, if you lead. Again, none of this tells you whether he is into you (for you) or not. Let him lead. That way, you KNOW where you stand. It always works best that way.

Think about it. It's human nature. People want what they can't have. If he wants to be around you more and he can't have you (because you have to leave), he will only want you more. Follow me? Good.

Here is another reason why I have this short-first date rule…doing something different makes you remarkable and memorable. Practically ALL women want a long first date. They want a fancy dinner, or maybe dinner and a movie, or dinner and theater tickets. When I make a short, first date, they are in SHOCK. You stand out. Listen to me! You stand out! I don't do it for that reason, but heck, let me say it again, You Stand Out. It makes them take notice. It sets you apart because you are not doing what all the other women are doing. He gets to thinking, "Gee, why is she doing this? What's she got?"

Any upstanding gentleman at this point will be begging you to let him take you to dinner, the concert, or whatever five hour date he can muster. While this is very flattering, don't take the bait. By the way, it is perfectly ok by me to have the second date be long. He can do these nice outings on the second date, not the first. (Don't tell him all this! You keep the power to yourself. By telling him your tactics, he may see this as game playing and dump you on the spot. I know. I was an idiot once and spilled the beans and lost a terrific guy in one second. He took what I said out of context and immediately dumped me.)

When you politely decline his offer (for a long first date), it ups the ante even more. He is now thinking, "I'm throwing money at her and she's not going for it? Wow. What an unusual girl!" After complimenting you in his head because he is keeping score by the way, he then turns the situation to himself (as most guys are self-centered) to say "Wow. Maybe she is going out with ME, to get to know me, and not my money or what I can do for her." More points are racked up. Feel me?

He also is impressed you are standing your ground. Most men worry you are going to cheat on them. Men don't take well to cheating. It takes them years, if not forever, to recover. Knowing a girl stands her ground makes him think of you in a whole new light. (Bingo! Marriage material!) This is how a man interprets your standing your ground…"When I am not with her, and if a guy approaches her, she will stand her ground to ward off his advances." Any guy loves this quality in his woman. No man wants to feel insecure that you will cheat on him. A woman who knows how to say "no" is a woman he wants. Period.

So, how do you decline? Say "Gosh, I would love to spend more time with you/go to dinner with you/go to the concert with you. Let's just meet at 7pm as planned. We can always do those things another time." Smile. Then, shut up. Be done with the conversation, politely, of course.

What is the perfect first date? Number one on my list is to go for a drink. One or two glasses of alcohol often relaxes people to be themselves and open up. The best time to go is before dinner, like happy hour, 4-7pm or after dinner, 7-9pm. If you or he don't drink, so what? That person can always just have a club soda or soft drink.

My second choice is to go for a walk. Maybe get an ice cream (or not) and go for a walk on the beach, a walk around the park or lake, a walk at the farmer's market, a walk around the grounds (like a rose garden or museum). If something grabs your attention, going on a walk is a great conversation starter. "Gosh, did you see those pears (at a farmer's market)? They were the biggest I have ever seen." "Gee, the birds are quite the singers today (around the lake)."

The cool thing about a walk is that you are close together but not in each other's face. He can be as casual or as intimate as he pleases. Here's how you KNOW you're doing it right: He takes your hand.

Other good marks: He walks curbside (the outside position, to keep you safe). He holds you back (nice, he is being a gentleman to protect you) when a car is passing. You can tell a lot about a man by how he walks with you.

Coffee dates? I love coffee. I have done coffee dates. Coffee dates, for me, almost never lead to a second date. A drink (alcohol) is almost always a sure thing. Coffee? Not so much. Also, coffee is usually in the morning. I usually have to be back at wor doing other things to start my day, meaning that I am w clock too much in the morning. If he is anything like me, to get on with his day, too (more clock watching!). Although coffee dates meet the one-hour date rule, they tend not to be productive.

Other ideas? If you happen to be athletic, men LOVE women who are athletic, by the way, hitting a bucket of golf balls is super fun. I got really good results doing this activity. Miniature golf, the shooting range at the local amusement park, and hiking up your local canyon are all good bets. Remember, if you are going to do an activity, you still have to keep it under one hour. Most men love to be active, so it's usually a good pick.

In summary, short and sweet gets the job done. If you can't see yourself with this guy physically or for other reasons, graciously let him go. If the date goes well, the anticipation of seeing him again will shine through. Everyone wants to be wanted. Your wanting to see him again will make him like you more because he is flattered that you like him.

Have fun. Here is one last tip, pretending that you have all the time in the world, keeps you in the moment. Being in the present, makes each of you show your real selves, which is what you want. That being said, get the heck out of Dodge when the time is up. Tick-tock.

My Notes:

My ACTION LIST:

Make Him the Most Important Person in the Room.

One of the most powerful tools in psychology is called Intermittent Reinforcement. The most famous use of this technique is Pavlov's dog experiment. He used a sound to initiate feeding time. With this sound, the dog began to salivate (to prepare his mouth for food). After successful salivation attempts, Pavlov decided that you don't even need to feed the dog. Just the fact that the dog heard the bell was enough for the dog to salivate.

How are you going to use this in real life? You're going to be busy. You're going to have a life in order to BE busy. You are not always available. Just like the dog's food was not always presented with each ringing of the bell, you are not going to be available every time your phone rings or the text alert is heard.

It is human nature for people to want what they can't have. You are in demand. Being sought after is incredibly sexy.

There is a fine line. In order for this technique to work well, it has to be intermittent, which means "some of the time." If you are consistently 'hard to get', that is an extreme, and he will go away. If Pavlov had never given the dog food again, no matter how many times he rang the bell, sooner or later, the dog would leave and go elsewhere for food. Got me?

So, when you are not together in person, be available some of the time, and sometimes, don't be available at all.

Here is the crucial part: when you are together, HE IS THE MOST IMPORTANT PERSON IN THE ROOM. That's the 'hook', that's the drug that will keep him coming back for more.

What does this look like?

- Put your iPhone not only down, but away. For twenty minutes while you're eating dinner, you can be unavailable to others. <u>That damn phone is not more important than he is</u>.

Unless the house is burning down, your grandmother just died, or a rare call from your boss, nothing is so important it can't wait.

- Mirror him. If he is playing with his swizzle stick, you play with your swizzle stick. If he's got his head cocked to the right, you tilt your head to the right. If he's got his right foot sticking out, you stick your right foot out. Mirror his body language.

  You're going to be cool about this. Don't make it obvious what you are doing.

  The reason why mirroring works is because it sends a subtle message that you "accept" and acknowledge him. This rapport means you're connecting with him and he will like that.

- Acknowledgment. Say "uh-huh" to acknowledge that you 'get' his point. You can even repeat what he said back to him, in slightly different words, just so he KNOWS you get it.

- Actively listen. Every now and again, clarify or have him expand on what he is saying. "That's a really interesting point." "Can you tell me more about that?" There are some men who pay for high-class call girls because these women are very good listeners. Some don't even have sex with them. Use this art to your advantage.

- Let him be the expert on something. If given the chance, men love to show off to you. "Wow, how did you *do* that?" "Can you show/teach me how to do that?"

- Touch his forearm. You have to do this like it's completely random. The forearm is the sole place on the body that gives a signal that you acknowledge/accept him. Also, it's a 'safe place' as the forearm docs not have an overt sexual connotation.

- Laugh at his jokes. Again, this means you acknowledge/accept him and are on the same page.

- Be present. Aside from the phone, clear your attention of other disturbances. If you're pissed about how your co-worker acted today, if you need to buy cat food on the way home, if you need to pay your insurance bill tonight, block those thoughts until you are on your way home.

If you find you cannot do some or all of these steps, he's not your guy. That's your red flag. I am not asking you to lie or be disingenuous. Don't date him if you cannot easily be in the moment with him.

Remember, when you're with him, BE with him. There is nothing more flattering to a guy than your being attentive and accepting of him. Nothing. Every guy wants to be the center of your universe.

If you do these steps, he will move mountains to want to see you more and eventually propose to you.

My Notes:

My ACTION LIST:

Be Slightly Disinterested.

The person who wants *something more* is the person who has less control/power.

Relationships work best when he takes the lead. It doesn't have to be a lopsided lead. It only needs to be by 1%. Let him like you at least 1% more than you like him.

Men work best when they get to hunt and chase. If you take that role, you come across as whiny and needy, which is a big turn off. If you find yourself getting edgy, antsy, and forward, pull back the reins. It's not going to work and your advances may even backfire to the point he dumps you.

The best way to be 'slightly disinterested' is to have a life, have other plans, and be busy. You are genuinely otherwise busy. That way, you don't have to lie or play games.

If it is in the early stages of dating and you are on your way to dating your 100 guys, it doesn't matter if *that guy* didn't call. You also went on three or four other dates this weekend. It is likely that one or more of them will call.

Most girls are SO EAGER to get into a relationship. Doing what 'most girls' do usually got me nowhere. On the other hand, approaching dating slightly differently than how most girls go about dating got me noticed, remembered, and called back.

How do you do accomplish this? Have options. If you're needy, this is the opposite of having options.

The combination that worked really well for me was my making him "the most important person in the room" (when I was with him) coupled with being "slightly disinterested" (when I was not with him in person). It basically sends the message that you are not going to live or die from his actions, that you are your own person…which is very alluring and sexy (from his point of view).

Let's recount. Being aloof and hard to get is rude and he is going to think you're not worth the effort. Being slightly, and the key word here is "slightly", hot (the most important person in the room) and cold, well, not cold, but more like cool (slightly disinterested) is what gets the job done.

Bottom line? When he likes you a tiny bit more, by at least 1%, than you like him, you have the control. This is not for you to misuse that control. Just keep it in check. It is *the knowing* you have control, but not doing anything with the unbalance of power that makes you worthy of his efforts.

My Notes:

My ACTION LIST:

Is He Off His Momma's Lap?

Something to consider when you have started to date is your man's living arrangements. Two potential warning signs of a man not ready to commit are:

a. If he is still living with his mother or
b. He is a serial monogamist

Run to the nearest online dating site and start again.

Why is this important? You want a grown man. If he is currently living with his mom or goes from woman to woman with no break, that is a red flag. Ideally, you want someone who has lived on their own for at least two years.

Why? When something spills, there is no one to look to and no one to blame. He has to get out the mop and clean it up himself. If the laundry piles up to the ceiling, it is not going to get done unless he hires a maid or does it himself. If there is nothing in the fridge, a responsible single man will eventually go to the market and learn to prepare at least three or four dishes.

Living alone requires a certain level of responsibility. You do not want to play mom or maid with someone who has no sense of obligation. It is a huge turn-off. You want someone you can respect and look up to.

Holding down a job, paying your bills on time, and renting or owning your own place all increase a man's sense of responsibility. Life will throw out many challenges. Whether the person can weather the storm, in large part, depends on how he has built his foundation. If he is no good to himself, he certainly cannot be of good use to others (you or his future family).

Being a responsible person matters. It speaks to a man's character. This is an easy area of character to detect but one that many women overlook. Don't let this easy check point slip under your radar.

My Notes:

My ACTION LIST:

Don't Tell Him What You Want.

"I want a relationship and babies." Save it. He's heard it a thousand times.

Are you really *that* self-centered that you have to state the obvious? Here you are having a perfectly fine first or second date and you're blathering on about how you want a 'relationship and babies'. Really? Here's the biology. Women are hard-wired to pop out a kid.

In 1970, only 10% of women were childless. In 2008, that number increased to 18%. The reason for this is because the invention of the Pill (in the late sixties and readily available to the public by 1973) women were able to delay or forego pregnancy in favor of furthering their education and/or careers.

This statement by women is boring, redundant, and obvious. Do not have this talk so early in the game. The first three months of dating should be light-hearted and fun. That's what draws a man into you, you are fun to be around. Having this talk too early in the game may cause a man to run out the door as he is not quite ready to process what you are asking (monogamy and children). He doesn't even know *if he likes you* and there you are blabbering on and objectifying him for sperm-donation purposes. How is that endearing or sexy? It's not.

Remember I said that women are fast and men are slow? It usually takes about three months for the guy to know if he wants a relationship with you. Can you have this conversation? Sure. Just delay it to the three month mark. The proper time to have this conversation is when you have his commitment.

If you are still not getting what I am saying, let me put it to you clear as day. The biological drive for women is to pop out a kid. The biological drive for men is to have sex (for the continuance of the species). Your saying you want a 'relationship and babies' is the equivalent of him saying he wants sex.

How would YOU like it if you're on a first or second date and your date says he wants to have sex with you? Your first reaction would be to say "ick" and your second reaction would be to say "duh". That's how you come across by having this conversation at this early stage.

Your goal here is to attract him not push him away.

How will you be alluring and captivating? Be cute, be chill, and be fun to hang out with.

My Notes:

My ACTION LIST:

Get Rid of the Extra Men in Your Life.

Start pruning the extra, heterosexual men in your life when you have a new man. It's ok to keep your gay besties, just weed out the other men in your life. They are cock-blockers. Your new man views any other (heterosexual) man as a cock-blocker. I know women can have male friends and just be friends (because we don't think of them in sexual terms), but men can't.

So that guy in your life is likely a guy who couldn't close the deal with you. He thinks if he helps you buy new tires or helps you paint your living room, that you are going to have sex with him. I know YOU don't think that way, but HE does.

He is also secretly jealous of any new man you bring into your life. As a result, you don't need your 'friend' to cock-block your new man.

If you want to stay single, ignore this step. Besides, you will inherit a pile of new men into your life as platonic male friends, your new man's best friends. So? How long are you planning to stay single before you take this step? Thought so. Good girl!

My Notes:

My ACTION LIST:

Don't Make Him 2nd Banana to Your Son.

If you are single and have a son, do not make the son the center of your universe in front of your new man (or for that matter, your permanent man).

The reason why you make your son the center of your universe is likely because his dad didn't get the job done. He didn't make you feel special or cherished. You then think that you are going to mold your son to be the man* your ex wasn't.

Do not do this for two reasons. Your son will grow up feminized and won't actually possess good male qualities. Secondly, don't do it because no new man wants to play second fiddle to some other guy, especially a teenage boy. All men want to be top banana in your life. The fact you have an inherent bond with your son is already a given. You don't have to rub this in your new man's face.

So? What does this mean? Hire a babysitter. Make plans for regular date nights. You don't have to have your son be part of every date. Your relationship with your new man will not fully mature like this. When you're on a date with your new man, don't talk about your son…at all. You can talk until the cows come home about your son to your mom, your best friend, your hairdresser, and whomever else you can muster up…just not your man. Is your son your reason for life? Well, ya. Would you die for your son? Of course! That being said, don't rub this in your new man's face. Is this going to be crazy-hard to do? Of course it is. But hey, you want to get married again, don't you? Just catch yourself while you're doing it. Conversations about your son should be kept below 10% of the time to your man. Like I said, there are plenty of people in your world with whom you can talk about your son…just not your man.

Also, for your own personal growth and development, you have to have areas in your life that do not include your son. Get a life! You will not only stunt your growth but severely limit your dating life if you make your son top banana.

Putting your son in the spotlight literally makes your son the *center of your life*. It blocks new opportunities (and men!) from coming into your life. Think this over and act wisely.

***The glorification of sons only happens with sons, not daughters. Moms do not glorify their daughters. Remember, she is trying to mold her son into what her ex was not. There is no point in doing this with a daughter as daughters are not "the man she wished she had".*

My Notes:

My ACTION LIST:

When to be a Lady. When to be a Man.

There are some characteristics about being a woman that are excitingly fascinating to a man. Here are a few most men really fall for:

- Giving him "the look".
- Flicking your hair.
- Walking with a swish.
- In a discreet, but not trashy way, not wearing underwear.
- Having that 'damsel in distress' look.
- Dropping something (that he comes over to pick up).
- Needing help (like picking up a heavy object).
- Licking something long, like a hot dog or lollipop.
- Slightly revealing (but not trashy) clothing that shows your breasts (if he's a boob guy).
- Leaning over with the much-awaited expectation of *possibly* seeing your boobs.
- Wearing clothing that shows your waist (hourglass figure).
- Clothing that shows your hips are sizably larger than your waist (if he's a 'hips' guy).
- Brushing your (long) hair.
- Applying makeup.
- Dressing in complicated undergarments: like stockings that have a line in the back, fishnet stockings, a corset, a garter belt, a bra that has a crisscross or some uplifting feature.

Here are a few things some women do that are typically male endeavors:

- Drinking beer.
- Smoking a cigar.
- Riding a motorcycle.
- Driving a pick-up truck.
- Driving a stick-shift.
- Driving a hot sports car (especially if it's a convertible).

- Really understanding a football game.
- Engaging in a sport that is typically a male sport.
- Lifting weights. Since most women don't even work out, let alone lift weights.
- Being physically good at something. Since most women are emotional, you will stand out if you physically excel at an activity.
- Being able to read maps and/or give (accurate) directions.
- Being good at math and/or science.
- Being well-versed in history, current events, or politics.
- Shooting a gun.
- Using power tools.
- Something that requires precision, focus, and a steady hand (like working on machinery, woodworking, artwork, or medical/dental).
- Being on-time (since many women are miserably late).

Be a little bit of both (male and female attributes) and do so randomly and unexpectedly.

Men are *fascinated* with female traits because they are so foreign to them…and, in some regard, they are kind of expecting (and wanting!) you to be different from them.

So, here's the deal. I am not going to lie…doing male activities has worked <u>very well</u> for me. Second only to sex, men want a companion to do activities with. If you are not only down, but enthusiastic about doing at least one male thing, you are IN.

My girlfriend and I argued this point endlessly. She does the female list, and does it not only better than me, but excels. She does NONE of the male activities and claims she doesn't need to. I do the female activities, not as well as she, but I take a good stab at them. As for the male list, not only can I do one male trait, but I can do almost the whole list. (I only recommend that you do at least one.)

She can get *any guy* to not only come up to her but to date her. She is very sexy and alluring. I don't have as easy a time as she does.

She's never been married. I have. She's never gotten a proposal. I have had more proposals than I can count…til it's embarrassing, that I actually stopped going on more than two dates because the guys always propose on the third date.

Don't get me wrong. I am very much a girly-girl. I love lace, ruffles, pearls, heels, and dresses. That being said, I can absolutely say, having at least one male activity definitely gives you the home court advantage. If you are looking to not just date, but to get a proposal, having this compatibility definitely closes the deal. It works very well because it is unexpected. Doing something outside the norm will always give you an advantage.

Some women will lie and say that they enjoy a typically male-based activity to win over the guy. In my book, lying never works and will eventually catch up with you. Just keep looking until you find one activity you can get behind. All it takes is one.

To retain your edge, never brag about your prowess at a male-based activity. On the exterior, continue to be your delicate, little flower self. Only when the opportunity arises do you show your hand and actually engage in the male activity. In waiting for the correct moment, you will blow your guy (and his male buddies, if they are present) A-W-A-Y.

Doing the unexpected not only gets you noticed, it gets the job done. What guy *wouldn't* want to have a girl like that by his side? Go get 'em, cowgirl!

My Notes:

My ACTION LIST:

Men are Typically Not Talkers.

If you are a talk-a-holic, figure out a way to curb this obsession. Talk-a-holics are often very self-centered. Being in a relationship is give and take. There should be a balance of communication.

If you talk a normal amount (please confirm this with a male you trust), and he talks zero, that's a red flag. It's time to dump him. What differentiates us from the Animal Kingdom is our ability to talk. The strong, silent type only works for so long. After that, it's annoying…just like being a talks-a-lot is annoying.

***

Ok, let's say you have established that you are each participating in the conversation. Women tend to be long-winded and men usually like to get to the point. Understand this crucial difference. You both should strive to be in the middle. He needs to offer more than one word answers and you need to pare it down from four pages of text.

While we are at it, avoid giving men hints and clues. While women are experts at "reading between the lines' and "filling in the blanks", men aren't. Men's brains do not operate in this manner. If you need to convey something, do it quickly and to the point. That's how men process it best.

My Notes:

My ACTION LIST:

Seek to Understand, Then to be Understood.

This is one of my all-time favorite quotes from Stephen Covey's highly successful book 'The 7 Habits of Highly Effective People'. Both parts of this sentence impart such a valuable message. I firmly believe if more people abided by this principle, it would remove 99% of all communication errors.

The first part is to start by understanding the other person. Most people are so self-centered that they cannot even begin to consider the needs of others. They just have to get their agenda out first. By being self-oriented, you are stuck in your own head rather than actively listening to what the other person is saying. Successful people know, effective communication is not a one-way street.

If George Clooney were calling, you'd be straining yourself to hang on every word. If the President of the United States were calling, you would make every effort to acknowledge what this VIP was saying. Too much self-chatter will sabotage your efforts. Your man is (soon to be) the most important person in your life. You don't have to agree with his stance, you just need to acknowledge it. Being inclusive sends a message that you not only understand, but you respect his position. Don't underestimate the value of this lesson. All men will be naturally drawn to women who respect his position.

Most couples break up because of:

- Sex
- Money
- Communication

Actually, that's not entirely true. In order to solve a sex or money issue, you have to communicate. It is then reasonable to conclude most couples break up because of a breakdown in communication.

Not really listening leads you to either jump to conclusions or assume he said *this*, when he really meant *that*. Either way, it's not a smart game plan. If you are not capable of listening to your partner at that moment, politely say "I'm in the middle of something. Can we table this for 30 minutes/until 8pm (or whenever your soonest immediate opportunity is that you can give him your full attention)?"

How do you know you are doing this right? Before you actually get into the conversation, repeat or paraphrase what you think you heard: Then say, "Is that right/correct?" When you get a confirmation, then you can proceed.

The second part of this sentence is when you are done discussing the issue, to make yourself be heard/understood. Women can usually tell if their guy is getting it by their body language or tone. Most men (unless they are left-handed*) do not have this ability. That's ok. They can use the 'request and confirm' step in the previous paragraph.

If your man is absolutely not getting the gist of what you are saying, it's ok for the woman to resort to the 'request and confirm' step, too. It might go something like this "Just so we are clear, can you tell me why you think *I'm upset* on this issue?" Usually at this point, the men are finally listening because men don't like to be wrong.

Avoid using the words he "got it wrong" as he will get side-tracked *on that*, rather than the issue at hand. Instead say "Oh, I see the confusion. Here is why I got upset." Then go into it, briefly and get to the point.

**Left-handed men have brain structure than is similar to female brains. Most women can cross the Corpus Collosum, the bridge between the left (logical) and right (emotional) brain easily. Left-handed men also have this ability. This exception only applies to men as left-handed women have no difference in their brain capabilities when compared to right-handed women.*

Since women are typically raised to be people pleasers, I know it is very hard for them to not only actually speak up, but to get their needs met and be understood. The first part of overcoming this is being acutely aware during each conversation. The second part is to actually put it into practice, which is why I am giving you actual lines (from the previous page) to use (until you come up with ones that feel natural to you).

Communication is only 7% verbal and a whopping 93% non-verbal. So watch your body language, your tone, your grunts, sighs, etc.

How do you know he is a good guy? He will make you feel safe. Feel safe to open up, no matter what the topic. If he is quick to anger or still not listening to you, you will have to toss that fish back in the sea! It's a big red flag.

Communication, or lack thereof, is a very good indicator if you two will not only last, but if you will last contentedly.

Couples who last are those who 'get' each other. Communication is open, loving, respectful…and fun! Looks and sex may fade one day. Finding someone who has your back and you have theirs is everlasting. Look for these traits.

My Notes:

My ACTION LIST:

A Smart Girl is an Irresistible Girl…Long Term.

Fact: Women with higher education are more likely to marry than women with less than a college degree.

The main reason that guys have sex with you is because you are hot. Just because they have sex with you doesn't mean they will want you as a girlfriend or propose to you. Yes, they are attracted to you because of your looks. Don't let it end there. And in case you haven't noticed, looks fade, so you're going to have to bring more to the table than just looks.

Beginning in my 20's and continuing on into my forties 40's, I woke up an hour early to read the paper…every…single…day. Now (post-internet), I have all my favorite news sources on Twitter feeds. I click and open stories of interest me, in addition to all the other reading I do during the day. I am not going to ask you to read for an hour a day, but at a minimum, read four articles a day. On average, each story takes about three minutes. Anyone can spare 12 minutes, so get to it.

I want you to read two front page stories, one story from the business page, and since most men love sports, read one story from the sports page.

No, women's subjects do NOT count toward this total. Reading about your favorite reality star, fashion, or other 'girl' topics don't count. You can read girl topics, they just won't count in your total. Most men could care less about women's topics. You have to read in areas that overlap with their interests.

12 minutes is so doable. You don't even have to read in succession. You can read while in line, pumping gas, or even on the john. You have to bring more to the table than just your body. Interesting people read. Get to it.

My Notes:

My ACTION LIST:

If You Can Control Him, Dump Him.

I know we women don't consciously set out to control him, but we control him just the same. I want you to raise your awareness in this area. If you find yourself controlling him, he is NOT the right match for you. The bottom line of *why* you do this is because you don't respect him.

You cannot fully love someone you don't respect.

You must let him go. He is not a fixer-upper. Either you trust and respect him or you don't. It is just that simple.

Keep looking. You will thank me later when you find the guy you trust and respect. By trusting and respecting, you are allowing him to be the man. You are allowing him to take charge and get it done. The more you allow this, the more of a true man he will be. It is just that magical.

If you don't focus on him, you will free up countless hours of nitpicking and nagging and instead have moments that bring you closer together. And don't you want to spend your days feeling close to your man? Loved by your man? Yes, you do. If you don't, this obsession is likely <u>your issue</u> and you need to get therapy to clear the cobwebs of your behavior.

Here's how you KNOW he is the one: you stop controlling him.

Stop controlling and be loved.

My Notes:

My ACTION LIST:

If You Can't Root for Him, Let Him Go.

It's been said 'Behind every good man is a good woman.' If you can't root for him, let him go.

This is another red flag for you (if you can't).

He is not a fixer-upper. If you find you have to do a major overhaul on him, he is not your guy. No guy wants to be taken over, controlled, or manipulated by a woman.

While I was dating my 70 guys, there was one guy I really liked and we had a good time together. The day after the date (which killed me, by the way, because he had a lot that was good about him), I told him I couldn't date him any longer. He asked "why?" He spent the better part of the evening bitching about his boss. Now I realize, we all have bad days. I realize many of us have bosses whom we don't like. The reason I couldn't date him was because it seemed like he was not only trapped, but that just talking about it was enough.

A bad situation is not bad.

What is bad is that he was not motivated to alter the ending to his story.

When he asked "why?" I said, "Because you spent a fair amount of time bitching about your boss. If you bitch about your boss, it will eventually backfire on me. It will rub off on how you treat me."

OH…MY…GOSH. He then proceeded to start World War III. He read me the riot act!!! He said "Who the hell do you think you are?? You barely met me. You don't know what responsibilities I have at work. You don't know how long I have worked there. You don't know whether I am proficient at my job. You don't know what type of person this boss is."

On and on, he was screaming. I had to hold the phone away from my ear lest I get tinnitus or something.

I said "You're right. I don't know any of those things. All I know is if things are as bad as you say, it will eventually (negatively) affect me."

He slammed the phone down.

Interestingly enough, he called me back in three days! He said no one has ever talked to him like that. He apologized for blowing up at me. He said it was a life altering moment for him not to hide behind his not liking his boss.

He called again three months later. He said he quit that job. He got another job that paid $25,000 more. He said he now loves his boss and it's a joy coming to work each day. On top of that, he thanked me from the bottom of his heart for being a stick of dynamite to change things for the better. …Aw!

We became very good platonic friends for years after that phone call. He called one last time, about three years later. He told me he just got married to the best girl ever and he thought it best that we don't talk anymore. I wished him well. I was SO happy for him.

As hard as it was for me that initial day to say I didn't want to be with him, the story had a happy ending. Here is another red flag: Don't be around someone who is stuck. Being stuck has drama, and sooner or later, you will be sucked into that drama.

***

So, how do you be his cheerleader?

Figure out or talk about what his hopes and aspirations are. Then work with him to support his goal. Just like you want your team to win, you want HIM to win. It might be changing his job. It might be something on his bucket list. It might be a degree or certificate. It might be getting some acknowledgment or accolade from the community.

Don't bad mouth his dreams. Don't say "That's ridiculous" or "You'll never amount to anything". If you really feel that way, you should leave him.

You have to find ways to support his dream…for real and wholeheartedly. Do you have any idea what kind of drug that is to him?? Winning your admiration and respect means everything to a guy. Many goals are really hard to obtain. Most men would get there quicker by having a good woman by their side. If he associates you with what is good about his life, there is no doubt that he will have you IN his life, and permanently.

Here's some pom-poms. Get to it.

My Notes:

My ACTION LIST:

Never Ask "What are We?"

A lady never asks. She doesn't have to. You can't ask because you will take on the role of the male. You don't want to be the guy, you want HIM to be the guy. If you are the guy, he won't do it.

I know you are going to say, "This is so old-fashioned. It is the next millennium. Of course girls ask the guy this question." To that I say, it might be the new age, but biologically speaking, not much has changed in tens of thousands of years.

If you do it, if you come forward, he won't.

For that reason alone, you should not come forward. You want HIM to be the guy.

Are you curious? Yup. Do you want to know? Of course. Are there ways to find out? Yes, indeed. But you cannot be the guy and be direct about it.

You can…but it will backfire.

Why are you so antsy? Because no one taught you how to be a lady and feminine. You were brainwashed into thinking that the sexes are the same and it shouldn't matter who asks and when.

Phooey!

Can you get what you want? Of course. Every true woman knows her power. Of course you can get what you want. Being direct is male energy. You want to use your female power which is "to wait". To wait is very powerful. It is the same energy as veto power, the power to say "no". Although it seems counter-intuitive, there is great power in "waiting".

The person who 'waits'/YOU/women have the power. It is the person who 'approaches'/HIM/men who take the risk.

It's kind of like going on an interview. There comes a point in time where the interviewee should just shut up (like the time when salary is discussed). He who talks first is the one who is at risk. The one who evaluates the offer is the one who has the power (veto power) to say 'yes' or 'no'.

So, how do you get what you want? Zip it! Never be the first one to ask/say:

- I love you.
- What are we?
- Will you marry me?

Why not? Because men are slow. You have to acknowledge that men are slow. It usually takes most men 3 months to have these feelings bubble up. We already know that women are quick. Women take anywhere from 5 minutes to 3 weeks to develop such feelings. Call it, we are more (emotionally) evolved than men. The sexes are not the same. So what? Just because YOU are fast, doesn't mean HE is. You have to respect that. You have to honor HIS timetable or you will be drop kicked to the curb…or lied to. Neither of which is what you want.

So, you:

- Love him
- Know you want him
- Know you want to be in a relationship with him
- Want to marry him.

What should you do? *This is the point where you get out your yellow highlighter...* What should you do? ACT AS IF you don't care.

Gosh, how are you going to pull that off? Get a life. A good woman is busy. If you don't have a full life, that's 90% of your problem right there. Let me say it again, it's YOUR problem that you are feeling antsy. When you are idle, it is easy to fall into the trap of being too focused on him, which is not attractive. By being busy, you won't even notice the time has passed and he will come around when it is natural for him.

The more you don't care what he does, the more he will want you. No guy on Earth wants a girl who is clingy and needy.

Girls who are laid back are confident girls. (You KNOW he will eventually come around. There is power in that!) You 'let' him come around and profess his feelings for you. Coming around first is gauche and not lady-like.

How are you going to handle this 'waiting around'? Well, I'm going to tell you the timetable for men.

- I love you. For men, it usually takes 3 months.
- What are we? For men, it usually takes 3 months (to be in a relationship).
- Will you marry me? For men, it usually takes 1 year to know.

Wait, isn't the name of this book, "Hitched. In 90 days or Less"? Yes, if you follow the rules of this book, he will propose in 90 days. He doesn't want to lose you because you are so amazing, so NOT like all the other girls. He definitely needs you by his side.

If you break a few of these rules, the standard amount of time is one year to get the proposal.

Here's how you know you are not doing it right. He doesn't commit (i.e. he is still playing the field) and/or you two are 'dating' for years and years. You think he is 'commitment-phobic', you break up, and the next girl he meets, he marries.

***

"C'mon, Linda. You are being a dinosaur. It's perfectly ok if the girl asks the guy to be exclusive/marry."

I have interviewed over **20,000 men** (for my men's book, The Art of Mastering Women). I have talked to men who were proposed to by their woman. Some of these guys left (as they weren't feeling it) and some of these guys said "yes". Guess what? The ones who said "yes" usually did so because it was convenient, they were horny, lonely, bored, or they felt there was something to gain from the woman (i.e. she made more money than he did).

Yes, many of them did say "yes" to her proposal. For those who married, the marriage lasted 5, 10, or even 20 years. In each and every case, not only were they were not happy, most of the men cheated. In each and every case, he became such an a*hole that the woman left him (so he could then be free). I asked what he would do differently. Each and every one of them admitted they would have NEVER married this woman to begin with.

Do you really want a man who feels this way? Are you that desperate? If a guy isn't asking you to marry him, there is usually a reason…he doesn't want you. If that is the case, you should move on. If it's been a year, just move on. If it is meant to be, he will come around. If it's not meant to be, it is a blessing that you got out of that situation to free yourself up to someone who really does want you.

I know this is harsh, but this is how men think.

There is no such thing as a man being a commitment-phobe. He either wants you or he doesn't. If he doesn't want you, his actions are clear…he won't ask. BUT, he will ask the next woman after you to marry.

Out of the hundreds of guys I interviewed whose woman asked him to marry, there wasn't one case where this worked out. Not one.

Please don't be that desperate to be one of these women.

When a guy wants you, he wants you. Sure the 'normal' time for men is 90 days (for being in love/being in a relationship) and 1 year for the proposal. If the guy really wants you, he will come forward. In my experience, I have often experienced men who come forward, and come forward strongly, in 3 dates. I'm not setting the bar that high for you, but I'm giving you the range of what IS possible.

If you're the right woman…NOTHING will stop the guy from coming forward.

This book is about making <u>you</u> that 'right' woman.

My Notes:

My ACTION LIST:

One Sleepover Day. Don't Move In.

After having sex, I am going to allow you to sleepover only 1 day a week. I am calling this your One Sleepover Day per week day. You can have sex more often than that, of course…just don't sleep over. A sleep over is too comfortable for him. He is lulled into a stupor to not continue to vie for your love and attention.

You would rather he think "Darn. Where is she? I want to **be** with her."

Plus, you want to be in demand. You're busy. Friday night? Maybe you're out with the girls after work for happy hour. Saturday night? Sure, spend the night, but Sunday night, after a fun day, sleep in your own bed - alone.

Figure out ways to be busy so you won't be putting all your 'me-time' into his basket. Go out Friday, even have sex Friday after going out, then leave. "Gosh, I have to get up early because that 6am yoga class is killer!"

The exception to this rule is when you guys go out of town together. Then you can obviously stay with him the whole weekend. Second only to sex, men LOVE having a girl by their side to do activities. By only staying with him long term on vacations/getaways, he will really LIKE being with you and will figure out a way to be with you more…even if it means he has got to propose to you!

His buddies are great, but he figures men with men are one-dimensional. He likes YOU. You add so much more dimension to his life. He opens up to you in a way that he doesn't with the guys. To that end, if you are cute, chill, and fun to be around, he will find a way to propose.

***

Should you move in with him? NO. The old saying is correct. Why buy the cow when you already are getting the milk for FREE? NO.

He should be slightly annoyed that he doesn't have you around all the time. That's what is going to get him to act.

He tells you that he "wants to test the goods (move in) before proposing." That's just a load of male bull crap. A recent study on cohabitation concluded that after five to seven years, only 21 percent of unmarried couples were still living together. Conversely, 79% of cohabiting couples split up. Of the 21%, only about half (that's 10%) got married (see statistic below).

Do you really want only a 10% chance of getting married if you move in with him??

Cohabitating couples that were engaged to be married had a lesser chance of actually getting married than those who got engaged and lived separately.

- 55 percent of cohabitating couples get married within five years of moving in together.

- 40 percent of couples who live together break up within that same time period.

Living together is not all it's cracked up to be.

- Numerous researchers are finding that couples who live together have a higher rate of divorce than couples who don't cohabit before marrying.

- Female cohabiters have divorce rates that are twice as high as women who cohabited briefly just before marriage.

- And prior to the divorce, cohabiting couples have lower rates of marital satisfaction.

I will make an exception that you can live together one month out from your wedding date. That should be sufficient time to 'kick the tires' to see if the car still runs. Long cohabitation times lower your odds of:

- Getting engaged
- Getting married
- Staying married (researchers consider over 15 years as a successful marriage)
- And being happily married

Researchers say your odds at a successful marriage go down due to cohabitation because of the effect of "sliding, not deciding." Just because you sleep at each other's places, you like being together, it is cheaper and more convenient isn't reason enough to live together. You are there by default rather than making conscious and clear decisions about who you are as a couple and what you want.

***

Let's throw in one last deterrent to marriage: children.

The likelihood that a woman will eventually marry is significantly lower for those who first had a child out of wedlock.

- By age 35, only 70 percent of all unwed mothers are married.
- In contrast, 88 percent of women will marry IF they have <u>not</u> had a child out of wedlock.

I know it is very popular and common to live together. Cohabitation in the United States has increased by more than 1,500% in the last 50 years. In 1960, about 450,000 unmarried couples lived together. Now the number is more than 7.5 million. Just because it's common doesn't mean a smart girl should do it.

This book is to teach you how to better your odds, not how to knock down your odds. Just because living together is easy, convenient, and cheaper doesn't mean you should do it.

Don't cheapen yourself. Guys LOVE the chase. If you are too easy they aren't motivated to change the arrangement.

Save the 'easy, convenient, and cheaper' for marriage. You'll be glad you did.

My Notes:

My ACTION LIST:

You Need to NEED Him.

Ok. Stand up. Stretch. Get a glass of water. Then come back and sit down. This section is very important.

You need to NEED him.

I know, I know…your mom told you to "be independent, go to school, get a good job, and don't depend on a man." I'm not talking about the kind of dependence your grandmother likely had. This is a "modern day" NEED.

Good for you that you are strong. I wouldn't want it any other way. In the workplace, you can be Miss Amazon Woman. With your man, you have to make 'room' in your life for him.

In doing the research on my men's book, respectively, there are also four must haves for *women* to win over a man. They are innate, biological drives all men have irrespective or race, color, religion, geography, etc. I call them <u>DT's Men's Core 4.</u> They are (in this order):

1. NEEDED
2. ACCEPTED
3. APPRECIATED
4. RESPECTED

The number one desire of men is to be Needed. **Men must be NEEDED in order to feel love.** They need to feel useful, helpful, and worthy. That's my definition of the word NEEDED.

This is a very different word than NEEDY, which is generally a turn-off.

There must be a place, however big or small, in your life for him. If there is no such place, no matter how smart you are, how much money you have, how gorgeous you are, how talented you are, and so on…he won't stay. Within a few months' time, he will be gone.

Let me give you a couple of examples:

a. A high-powered female attorney 'took' (married) her man because he is a great chef and is into the arts. He softened that tough edge that she had at work all day long.

   He made a little less money than she did. When it came to work, she took on more of the masculine/breadwinner role. Taking on a masculine role at work is perfectly fine. Just don't bring on masculine energy when you come home with your man. Let him takeover.

b. The second woman was raised in a very strict background. It seems like all her parents wanted her to do was study to get good grades and practice the piano. "All work and no play make Johnny a dull boy", as they say. She let him in by making her laugh all the time. He had a great sense of humor, but it made him particularly happy to lighten his wife's load this way. He felt NEEDED and useful. Her parents were wrong. Every girl needs a little laughter in their day.

c. She is very regimented, he is very spontaneous.

d. She is on the computer all day long because she runs an online business. She married him because, unlike her, he is exceptional with computers. Since she uses the computer all day long, her computer often crashes and is subject to viruses. He has the golden touch fixing and maintaining her computers.

e. She's an actress and a good one, but struggles remembering her lines. Her partner supports her by helping with memorization. His patience and active role allows her to focus on acting rather than just stressing on lines.

I think you get the picture now. There has to be at least one thing that he's good at and you're not good at. He is bursting at the seams to do this thing for you. Back in your grandmother's day, we could say this conversation would relate mostly to money, i.e. she needed him to be the breadwinner. In today's world, it's not so much about money, as women are in the work force. There are a million and one ways that your guy can feel NEEDED.

Hopefully, with your man, you KNOW what that 'place' is, right off the top of your head. You KNOW why you keep him. If you want to keep him, but you don't know WHY, you had better try and figure it out, and quickly. The clock is ticking. He is trying to figure out why you NEED him. Sooner or later, he will run out of ideas. That's the moment he will walk.

If he is NOT trying to be useful for you, he is NOT a good guy. You need to dump him.

All men have this gene/drive. There are no exceptions. It's an inherent trait. If he is not giving to you in one way, even a small way, he is a player and needs to be dumped. He figures he has it so going on that he doesn't have to give. Ya, right. Next!!

If you can't think of ONE THING you NEED him for, YOU are a user, and it is YOU that needs to dump him. Cut him loose so he can be a good guy with someone else.

Wow, I'm impressed. Some of you figured out how this chapter is going to end. Nice work, grasshopper! This is another one of those things where it's more about YOU than him. Let's see if your feminine card is broken, yet again.

In order for you to NEED him, you have to yield, you have to let him in, and you have to surrender. There, I said it. Surrender. Remember, this is not your grandmother's day where she really did need him, financially and otherwise. The balance of power was lopsided, maybe 90-10. I'm talking today. I am talking about a more balanced scale of power. You're a capable woman. You only NEED to let him in by at least 1% for this to work. The relationship will not be happy or sustaining if it is completely 50-50. Understand? If nature wanted us to be completely equal, nature would have invented just one sex. There are two sexes for a reason.

You bring out the best in him by allowing him to be the man, lead, and give to you. He needs this element like he needs air. Just like you need him to be CONFIDENT. **He needs to be NEEDED to feel love.**

In order for him to love you, you have to let him … (fill in the blank).

So? Let him love you, my pretty. Let him love you.

My Notes:

My ACTION LIST:

Uh-oh. I Have Done Everything Wrong. Is There Still Hope for Me?

Yes, there sure is. It's never too late to start using these tips. JUST START NOW!

If you don't want to be with him anymore, move out. No drama. Just say you are done with the status quo and it's time to move on. Sleep on your friend's couch. Move back to your parents' house. Start a move-out fund, however small, $100 a month or whatever you can afford. Just do it. Cut out all disposable spending (like going to Starbucks). Your entire focus should be to leave the situation. Give yourself a hard deadline to leave…and do it.

If you want to keep him?

- Use my tips to be irresistible.
- Start practicing the art of saying "no". You can practice on your friends, family, and co-workers. That way it will be easier to say to him.
- Smile. Make a practice of smiling at least once per hour, even if no one is watching. Hang a mirror over your desk and practice!
- Be receptive to his advances.
- What's blocking you? Move those hurdles out of the way!
- Hit the 'reset' button. Change your routine a bit.
- Make room in your life for him. Is there a corner or two in your home that is "man-friendly"? Get rid of the pink bedspread and make it more neutral. Get 2 end tables, 2 lamps, and/or hang a picture with a couple dancing or

walking together.

- Stop wearing so much black. Pull out 5 colorful tops and wear one each day.

- Define what you like. Only be with someone you are proud of.

- If you are dating someone at work, transfer to another branch or location, or if feasible, completely stop talking to him at work. If you must work together on projects, don't talk about anything other than something that is directly related to the work the two of you are doing. Don't talk about office politics or gossip. Don't talk about how you have this project and he has that project. Unless you absolutely must interact on the same project, don't talk at work.

- If you have moved out, are not currently living with him, or you dumped him, sign up online and by the 1st of the month, start dating your 100 men.

- If you're on the dating scene, keep your first date under an hour.

  If you are dating him, make sure you look good. Spruce up when you/he comes home. Brush your teeth before you see him.

  When you go out, make the extra effort to look good. If you normally wear your hair up, put it down. If you normally wear your hair down, wear it up. If you always wear jeans, wear a dress. If you always wear business attire, wear a white t-shirt or a button-down and jeans.

  If at home, dump those sweatpants and your favorite t-shirt with the hole in it.

Once a week, do housework with nothing but sexy lingerie and your best heels. Ignore him while you are doing said housework. Bend over every now and again. Stand on your tippy toes to reach something (to elongate your legs).

- Make him the most important person in the room when you see him.

- Be slightly disinterested in him when he's not around.

- Where is he living? It matters.

- Stop talking cold turkey about commitment and babies.

- Stop talking to other heterosexual men.

- I know it will kill you but make him more important than your son. How will you know you are winning with this? He will be good for you AND your son. You don't have to go this alone.

- Do the unexpected. Learn at least one male activity.

- If you have something important to say, practice before he gets home. Practice in the mirror or write it down. Don't spring it on him right away when he gets home. Men need at least 30 minutes of decompression time before they think of anything heavy again. Say it directly, say it simply. Get to the point. Keep your tone monotone. No drama. Monotone!

- Listen, then get him to listen back. Rather than outlining in your head what your next statement is going to be, actively listen to what *he* is saying first. As for you, when it's your issue to discuss, force yourself, calmly and in a monotone way (i.e. without sarcasm or hysterics) to make yourself understood. Practice talking quickly, quietly, and by getting to the point sooner than later.

- Improve your communication skills. Rather than outlining in your head what your next statement is going to be, actively listen to what *he* is saying first. As for you, when it's your issue to discuss, force yourself, calmly and in a monotone way (i.e. without sarcasm or hysterics) to make yourself understood. Practice talking quickly, quietly, and by getting to the point sooner than later.

- Start reading 12 minutes a day! Books, magazines, or online magazines. It doesn't matter which.

- If you can't stop controlling him, dump him. You don't respect him.

- If you can't find anything to support his dream or goal, dump him. You don't respect him.

- If he hasn't said "I love you" yet, don't you say it ever again. Let him come forward first. Don't ask what type of relationship you guys have. If you are that uncomfortable/insecure about it, leave. If he hasn't proposed, don't ever bring it up again.

  Start using birth control and/or condoms 100% of the time. You heard me. 100% of the time. Having a baby and not being married will only hurt, not help, your chances for marriage. Plus you're being selfish by not thinking what is in the best interest of your unborn child.

- If you live apart, only stay overnight one night a week. If you live together, change the routine. Go to bed earlier or later than he does. Do something different from what you are doing now. If it's early enough in the day, when you have sex, get up and get out of the house like it's on fire. I don't care if you leave to get coffee, go to the market, or leave to rent a movie. Just get out of the house. Don't snuggle, don't spoon, don't bathe together. Just get the heck out of the house. If you have plans with a girlfriend, all the better.

- If you don't already know, figure out what you NEED him for. Then, allow him to do it for you.

Bottom line? Just change things up. Being different will cause him to look at you differently. By all means, keep this to yourself. It is not his place to know what you're up to…only that you have changed. Your changing will cause him to act/react to you in a different way.

My Notes:

My ACTION LIST:

Be Magnetic.

It's feminine energy to attract/be magnetic. It's male energy to come forward/act. (Let him be the guy, damnit!)

Be magnetic. It's not brain surgery. All you have to do is do these three things:

1. Be cute.
2. Be chill.
3. Be fun to hang out with.

Happy dating!

Please send your engagement/wedding announcements to:
info@datingtipsforme.com

Contact

For signed copies, inquiries, or to send wedding invites:

Contact: info@datingtipsforme.com
www.datingtipsforme.com

For signed copies, please put "Signed copy" in the subject line.

Other Books by Linda Gross.

1. **Mastering Women.** The Definitive Guide to Understanding and Being Effective with Women.

   Ms. Gross interviewed over **20,000 men** to research what issues men want answers to regarding women. Many men today are at a great loss with how to interact with women. She brings them from being cocky and confused to CONFIDENT with women. Ms. Gross empowers men to tap into their innate skills to be effective in winning over women.

   Although the book is written for men, women benefit from reading the book as it is a perfect mirror on women's behaviors and how these behaviors affect men. The female reader can then take steps to correct behaviors that sabotage her and improve her relationships with men.

   http://www.amazon.com/dp/B00B0594II/?tag=dt4m-20

2. **The C Factor.** How to Get Anything You Want from Anyone. Mini-book (3 pages).
   This small but powerful book can be used in business or to ask even a perfect stranger for a favor.

   http://www.amazon.com/dp/B00BRYF3EG/?tag=dt4m-20

3. **365 Things I Taught My Teenage Daughter.** Coming soon.

   Everything you need to know to get started in life that they didn't teach you in school.

   www.amazon.com/author/dt4m

Closing Note.

Thank you for sitting down with me to read 'HITCHED in 90 days or Less'. Before you go, please take a moment to share, tweet, and rate this book. Your words mean the world to me. I look forward to speaking to you soon. DT

- Spread the word. Share this book with as many ladies as you can.

- Help others find me. Take a moment to review the book. 'HITCHED in 90 days or Less':
  www.amazon.com/author/dt4m

  Scroll down to 'Customer Review'.

About

Ms. Gross has a degree in Psychology from UCLA. She has hosted a weekly cable TV show, is a co-host and guest on dozens of radio shows, and was a top-ten blogger for several years. She offers one-on-one consulting as well as seminars.

She lives in Los Angeles, California with her family.

Excerpt from "MASTERING WOMEN".

The Definitive Guide to Understanding and Being Effective with Women.

I have given you all the instruction you will need on how to find your man in this book. Please do not read the section below for at least 24 hours. I want you to digest the valuable information you have read so far.

I am including this excerpt here because it speaks to why men are drawn to you. Men need to have these four points covered for them to take the next step with you (and eventually propose).

This chapter will give you an insight to how *men feel love.* The way men feel love is decidedly different than the way YOU feel love.

If you are interested in finding out how *your behaviors affect men*, you might want to pick up my "MASTERING WOMEN" book.

Enjoy,

DT

XIII. Men's Biological Drives.
DT's Men's Core 4.

DT's MEN'S CORE 4: The Chalkboard Formula

1. NEEDED
2. ACCEPTED (sometimes I call this one VALIDATION)
3. APPRECIATED
4. RESPECTED

Men's Core 4 Defined.

Based on my research in interviewing **20,000 men**, the following Core 4 Needs consistently made the top ranking for men (as the woman's list is very different). These 4 key characteristics are repeatedly mentioned by men that make men joyful and happy.

DT's MEN'S CORE 4:
1. NEEDED
2. ACCEPTED (sometimes I call this one VALIDATION)
3. APPRECIATED
4. RESPECTED

The "Men's Core 4" and "Women's Core 4" (The 4C's) are the crux of my research here. We have talked at length about the Women's needs earlier in the book. In this chapter, we will bookend those findings with the Men's Core 4 needs. You can apply these 4 tenets (respectively) not only to improve your relationship with her, but they are Universal Truths that can be applied to life in general.

1. **NEED:**

- You matter.
- You're essential to her.
- You're useful.
- You're bigger/better/smarter/faster/stronger than she, meaning that there is a quality you have that she needs that she cannot do for herself. You complement her. You fill in that which is a weak point/void for her.

2. **ACCEPTANCE:**

- She allows you to come over to her table.
- She allows you to talk to her.
- She allows you to enter her body.
- She has to yield to you.
- She has to let you take the lead. This trait is a very deep one, especially for today's modern, powerful women. This trait is really a sign that she's into you.

- She has to generally approve of your personality, attitude, your sense of humor, appearance, scent, hygiene, morals, etc.

Sometimes I call this Core Need: VALIDATION.

3. APPRECIATED:

- A man needs other people to recognize the quality, significance, or magnitude of his actions.

4. RESPECT:

- Honored. Held in high esteem.
- Valued.
- Possessing excellence.
- Having importance.
- Admired.
- Having others defer to you.

There you have it. Thousands of men complain that everything is great until the kids come. Now you have a reference guide for what makes you happy. When it goes off track, you can easily see where it derailed, and take measures to correct it.

You Both Cannot Lead the Dance.

With the exception of sex, you don't really need a woman. You take a woman because you WANT one. At no time in our history has this been more true than today (because sex is so readily available).

For a man's psyche, it's about building blocks. When you're ready to take a woman, it's about making sure she is doing the Men's Core 4 traits.

For her to implement all four of these traits - NEEDED, ACCEPTED, APPRECIATED, RESPECTED - she must give up at least a thumbnail's worth of control.

While it is a lofty goal to aspire to, with all the psycho-babble today that the sexes are equal, our hormones don't think they are equal at all. To that end, that is why relationships still work best when the man leads and she follows. It doesn't have to be lopsided like it was in our father's or grandfather's time, when those men did 90% or more of the work…but, it DOES have to be slightly, if only by 1%, led by the man.

'Follow?' She shrieks. Today, it's less about her following or submitting and more about you taking command and showing your CONFIDENCE, 1st C.

For most women today, to truly **yield** to a man is a very dicey matter. Over the past 40 or so years since Women's Lib, many women have been taught to "do it all yourself" because "you cannot rely on or trust a man". It is a particularly hard step for strong, independent women to take. Over 80% of the time, the woman doesn't want to yield. What is even more appalling is that as women get stronger and more educated, men become weaker and less educated. College enrollment for men in the last eight years has dropped off decidedly. It is the first time in our history where more women than men have applied to colleges. Men now trail women in college enrollment by 14%. So, what is there for her to do but take matters into her hands and control you? Much like training a dog, she will try to womanize you, make you adapt to female ways, and then reward you for compliance. Good Dog!!! However, as time passes, there is no way a woman can continue to respect such a man.

In Caveman times, it was female energy submitting to her man. You both cannot lead the dance. One person must lead and it often works best if it is the man. That's how nature intended it. Even if it's only by a very small margin, it works best if the man leads in the relationship by at least 1% or more of the time compared to the woman. It becomes increasingly difficult for a woman to yield to her man if he is not stepping up to take on this role. If he's not doing it, someone has to pick up the slack. It seems that today, women are stepping into this role more and more often. It can work for a short period of time, but sooner or later, she will resent him for not leading; resentment turns to anger; and that anger will turn into unpleasant or destructive behavior that is taken out on her mate.

When a man allows a woman to take the lead in the relationship, it will only work temporarily. Deep down, she will harbor resentment, demonstrate great levels of manipulation (because she can), and maybe even seek a new partner because this guy isn't "man enough".

Bottom line? You have to first become the person you want to be in order to attract the person you want to be with. That is Universal Law. You walk, she follows. That's how it works.

Be Needed, Not Needy.

Men's Core 4: 1st NEED.

If the woman doesn't see you fitting into her life for a specific reason, she will likely pass on you now or dump you later. Either way, it ain't pretty. Don't be a fool to think you can skip this step in finding how you are NEEDED. You cannot.

And you cannot take the easy way out and just ask her, either. Besides, **women often don't even have a clue what they need** (she 'cannot see the forest from the trees' syndrome). With an outsider's perspective, you can often see the NEED more clearly than the person who is living it. You're the logical one. Figure it out! Make it your business to determine what her need is.

When you discover on your own what she NEEDS, you're the hunter, which is how it should be. When you're in command, you can focus on what needs to get done. Otherwise, if you wait around for her to tell you what she wants/Needs, there is too much risk that she will just lie, manipulate, or abuse you.

You must find what her blind spot is, and fill it. Not only that, it should be something you're good at (and if you're really good at it, all the better) and she's NOT good at.

For strong, independent women getting this NEED met can be challenging. These women are so capable, they don't need anything in their life, or so they say. You have to realize that they have their shield up. Who cares? You're the man here. Shields can be broken. You have to zero in on what her weak area is and use it to capture her heart.

When you find her need, you are doing so for benevolent reasons, to be an asset in her life. This is not an exercise in exploitation which would be a Player move. Always keep your intentions honorable.

You have to be a sleuth of sorts. Figure out the NEED yourself and don't tell her HOW you fill that NEED. Just do it. A magician never reveals his secrets. It's like that.

Here are some examples of filling a NEED:

- You are more organized than she. You help her get and stay organized.
- You are more punctual than she. You keep her on time.
- You are more social than she. She counts on you to get her out of the house.
- She is more 'big picture', you are more targeted.
- She is often on an emotional roller coaster and you have a calming effect on her.
- She's the serious one. You bring humor to the table.
- She's the creative type. You're the one with business contacts to help her achieve her goals.
- Her schedule is very rigid. You bring spontaneity.
- No matter what kind of day she has had, you give her a hug and assure her that 'things will be alright'.
- She is more routine. You bring the 'fun'.
- If she's the major breadwinner, you make sure you bring the bread (i.e. you're the cook in the family and you feed her).

The overall disposition I'm looking for with this core need is that you in some way complement her – you fill a void in her life. In no way does this core need mean 'needy'.

Some way, somehow, she NEEDS you. Once you figure out what that is, you're golden.

Be the cream to her coffee. Got me? That's how you guarantee your position.

Why Being Needed is Important to a Man.

Let's define this term from your end, as well…Men's 1st Core tenet, NEED. I am speaking at a very deep level. I know this concept will be misconstrued by some. I am NOT referring to "Neediness". Men are hunters. Men are providers. It is in a man's inherent nature to provide. Men have to feel like they are NEEDED (useful). Of course, these are modern times and women are more capable now than ever before. That being said, in some form, men still need this core tenet satisfied. It may have to be tweaked to fit our current times, but it still must be present.

When I talk about being NEEDED in this context, it fits into the higher cognitive concept of Interdependence – meaning that you each "depend" on the other for something that you cannot do on your own (or that you just don't have inside of you).

Let's say one of you is the creative type and the other one is business minded and has the contacts to help make the artist successful. That's a good fit. OR, say one of you is either a tightwad or a spendthrift and the mate is good with budgeting and planning. That's a good fit. Finally, say one of you is prone to anxiety and the other has a calming effect. That's a good fit.

When a female reader asked me once why women should "need" a man and "isn't that a bad thing?" On a superficial level, yes, it's a bad thing. When you think of it that way, she was correct – a woman shouldn't need a man. However, when you get to the level I'm talking about, the (deeper) Interdependence level, then it makes sense.

The Men's Core 4 Traits are Successive.

1. NEEDED
2. ACCEPTED
3. APPRECIATED
4. RESPECTED

The Men's Core 4 traits are successive. Core 2 builds off Core 1. Core 3 builds off Core 2. And Core 4 builds off Core 3. Can these traits be present in a different order or can some be missing? Sure. While it is theoretically possible, it's not the best way to build a solid foundation. That breach of integrity/disingenuousness will sooner or later show up as a problem.

- A woman must have a reason for a man to be in her life (NEED).
- A woman must NEED a man in order to ACCEPT him.
- A woman must ACCEPT a man before she is able to APPRECIATE him.
- A woman must APPRECIATE a man before she is able to RESPECT him.

These actions are extremely hard for most women to do. Especially for a strong woman, it goes against her grain to yield to men in this way. Women feel threatened and vulnerable when they do them. They fear that they give up control. In fact…they do! Being in love IS A LOSS OF CONTROL.

The Men's Core 4 are very closely knit and intertwined. In order for a woman to do them for real, she must use her cognitive (human) abilities, not her biological animal drives.

Now that you know what the score is, you can spot a woman a mile away from one who is or is not doing these Core 4 behaviors.

She would only bestow these qualities on a man because she loves him (or in a work environment, for a man/boss she really admires.) It doesn't come naturally and she must put a great deal of thought into when she is going to submit to a man, which is precisely where you want her to be. You don't want someone who is hanging on and going through the motions just because she wants to "be in a relationship". You want her to make conscious decisions and single YOU out as being special.

You don't want her to stick around just because she wants to pop out a kid (her animal drive), meaning she could give a rat's ass about you. Many women, without even realizing it, are only with you because of their primal drive to pop out that kid. You are totally interchangeable with the next guy in line because she really hasn't given the relationship or you much thought. It may seem horribly blunt, but that is how it is.

Once you realize (dare I say it?) that it IS about Control and loss of it, you can flush out all her game playing around this issue. You can determine if she is real and if her intentions are honorable.

How Do You Know If You are Really in Love?

I often get asked "How do you know if you are really in love with a person, as in the 'you-would-do-anything-for-them' kind of love? From my extensive research on how women affect men, the following Core 4 Needs top the list for making men joyful and happy. These 4 traits are the recipe for how a man KNOWS he's in love:

DT's MEN'S CORE 4:

1. **NEEDED**
2. **ACCEPTED (sometimes I call this one VALIDATION)**
3. **APPRECIATED**
4. **RESPECTED**

If the woman is fulfilling the Men's Core 4, that's how you know she is a keeper. That's how you know you're in love. Getting these needs met is essential to a man. **It is so crucial to his well-being and happiness that if a woman does these 4 tenets, a man cannot help but to fall in love with her.**

I'm giving you the best cheat sheet ever!!!!

Damn, I'm good! Where else are you going to get a list of 4 simple traits that sum up whether a woman is worth your time long-term? (And Ladies, where are YOU going to get a list on how to win HIM over??)

Guys? If she is not doing ALL of them, you should ditch her, no questions asked - IMMEDIATELY!

These Core 4 Needs are Universal. I have put them to the test thousands-upon-thousands of times. They work for short or tall, fat or skinny, gorgeous or not so beautiful, dumb or smart, and they work across cultures, races, and religions. How do I know they work? Because my research strips away all the clutter and then further boils it all down to our pre-historic, core animal drives from 10,000 years ago – the Paleolithic period of human evolution.

I've sifted through over **20,000 interviews** to arrive at 4 simple words: One list for women, one list for men. And, the two lists are very different from each other!

You have great power over how your woman responds to you. Step into that power and quit acting like you don't have an effect. You set the tone. If you have the right energy, if you are giving, you will get back the love you give. It's male energy to give, and female energy to give back. If you are not getting the love you want, you should first look to see if you are really a giver because whatever you put into this relationship, you will get back. Actually, it's even better than that as we saw defined in a previous chapter. You will get back MORE THAN what you put in (her 110% to your 100%).

Sure, there are some men who take shortcuts, and through deceit, they win the girl. It won't last. It won't be the love of the century. Even though you may snow some women mentally, you won't snow her emotionally as she will always hold back a little and in order to fully win over a woman, you must win her over emotionally.

The Men's Core 4 are so valuable that never again will you have to ask "Did you miss me? Do you love me?" or whatever other current tactic you use. Even if she answers those questions affirmatively, she may not fully mean what she is saying because your question comes from a place of weakness and insecurity.

FLAT OUT:

- If she's not doing the Men's Core 4, move on. She's not your girl.
- If she IS doing the Core 4, she is definitely into you and is a keeper.

<u>That's how you know.</u>

How Do You Know for Sure She Loves You? (You must have all 4.)

DT's Men's Core 4:

1. She NEEDS you. You are useful to her in some way.
2. She ACCEPTS you. (i.e., She's not trying to change you. Here is the red flag, the things she is trying to change about you, SHE DOESN'T ACCEPT. Heed that as a warning.)
3. She APPRECIATES you.
4. She RESPECTS you.

You cannot ask for these traits from her. They are either there or they are not. Pay close attention. If you don't find her doing these things, SHE IS NOT IN LOVE WITH YOU.

Here is the bad part about women…

Will they talk to you? Yes.
Will they go out to dinner with you? Yes.
Will they date you? Yes.
Will they have sex with you? Yes.
Will they marry you? Yes.

None of these things mean squat to women. Women are supremely guilty for doing all of these things and STILL not giving a rat's ass about you.

Why would a woman do such a thing? There are a whole host of reasons: money, power, fame, bettering her social status, appeasing friends and family, on and on. Don't fall for it. Keep your eyes peeled for the Men's Core 4. If they are not present, move on.

There are plenty of women out there who think you're all that and are eagerly waiting to have you just the way you are. Don't settle!!! Get out and find her!!!